Crossing an Unseen Bridge

*The Law of Attraction Secrets
No One Wants to Talk About*

Patricia L. Arnold

PHOENIX IN PRINT
Chicago • New York

Copyright © 2008 Patricia L. Arnold

All rights reserved. Published in the United States by PhoeniX in Print. No part of this book may be reproduced in any form or by any means including electronic, mechanical or photocopying, or stored in a retrieval system without written permission from the publisher, except by a reviewer who may quote brief passages to be included in a review.

ISBN: 978-0-9761495-5-2

Cover design: Joseph Cabusao

Author photo: Eric Werner

Cover Photography: ©Andreyttl, ©Midhat Becar

Agency: Dreamstime

For Frances.
Life truly is Eternal.

Title is also available in audio book and ebook formats

Also by Patricia L. Arnold:

EARTH Is the Mother of All Drama Queens
Unmasking the Truth Behind Our Life Stories

For more information, visit:

www.patricialarnold.com
www.dramaqueenworkshops.com

Acknowledgments

My eternal love and gratitude to my teachers, muses and angels who have so generously, patiently and relentlessly walked this path with me, supporting my desire to fulfill my life's purpose. I am deeply indebted to Michael, Raphael, Gabriel and my earth angel, Maiysha. Without our partnerships, this experience would not be nearly as fulfilling, dramatic or joyful.

To the lovely group of seekers who helped me cross the bridge during the writing process: Meochia Blount, Ashley Brown, Michele Anderson Cabusao, Sonya Moore Lewis, Rhea Rhodes, Deborah Starr Seibel, Johnnie Swain, Natosha Walker, Melody Waller, Emma Young; and my brother-in-law and sister, Rodney and Dr. Helen Massey.

Thanks to the mega-talented creative geniuses who helped me manifest this project: Joseph Cabusao *(book jacket),* Christian Ericson *(website)* and Eric Werner *(author photo),* and to Lloyd Halsells, Earl Milloy and my baby girl, Maiysha Simpson, who moved at warp speed so that I could meet my audio book deadline.

A warm embrace to some incredibly supportive beings on my path: Lyle Banks, Ray Barbosa, Keith Boykin, Brenda Butler, Catherine Chiesa, Denise Collins, Merri Dee, the Rev. Vici Derrick, Russ Ewing, Dr. Elaine Ferguson, COL David Glover, Dr. Barbara Henley, Oliver Holliday, Doris Jackson, Ken Jones, Beverly Kennedy, the Rev. Dr. Barbara King, the Rev. Herbert Lassiter, Rosielyn Lassiter, Mimi and Dr. Ali Mafee, Ron Magers, America Martinez, the Rev. Gaylon McDowell, Jerry R. Mitchell, COL Thomas Nickerson, Lynn Norment, the Rev. Patty Pipia, Violet Ricks, Tony Shute, Bishop John Shelby Spong, the Rev. Shaheerah Stephens, Badriyyah and Abdul Waheed, Gail Walker, my big brother Gerald Walton, niece Rebecca Walton, aunt Georgie Warren, Lissa Woodson and my HIPP sisters: Gaile Dry-Burton, Patrice Gaines and Trevy McDonald. Finally, words cannot express how deeply I appreciate Rema Smith, who so lovingly and meticulously ensures that I don't appear in public with my "grammar slips" showing. *Love you, Girl!*

Prelude
Great Minds Think

This is not another "pour new wine into old skins" manual to help you create a more prosperous life. You will find no modern twists on ancient secrets here. There are no secrets, anyway. You already know everything you'll ever need to know. You've merely forgotten what you know. And yes, a part of you even knows that, too.

For whatever reason, you are convinced that others' wisdom is greater than yours, but all the wisdom you need is in your heart. You probably have conveniently forgotten because remembering means that you must take responsibility for getting your own answers, and you must be accountable for the situations and persons you attract into your life.

That's daunting.

No worries. A part of you knows that you have all eternity to remember. And at the most perfect time for you—not a moment too late or too soon—you will remember, and you will gladly accept the responsibility that comes with that memory.

If you have opened this book, it means that you are actively seeking the Truth about you. Have you noticed that you search for things you've lost with much more passion than you search for things you've never had? That's why your search has been so relentless.

You've followed many directions and encountered just as many roadblocks. Much publicity has surrounded those who have followed the same directions, performed the identical actions and have gotten the results they wanted, but you couldn't seem to make that quantum leap.

Frustrated and disappointed, you have persevered. Your determination has led you here, to the foot of a bridge that is mentioned in whispers.

Welcome! Soon you will be able to take a leisurely stroll across it, and take a shortcut to your Divine Destination.

Law of Attraction Secrets
No One Wants to Talk About

1. *Know Who You Are before Deciding What You Want*
2. *Understand Your Beliefs–and Their Implications*
3. *Act as if Life Is Round*
4. *Either the Law Controls Your Outcomes, or You Do*

"We can't solve problems by using the same kind of thinking we used when we created them."

Albert Einstein

Secret #1

Know Who You Are Before Deciding What You Want

If you're like most of us, you're perpetually searching for that elusive satisfied grin that symbolizes happiness. We read every new book and attend an endless array of workshops that promise turnkey solutions to improve our lives. We try to focus on positive thoughts as much as possible. Still, we only attract frustration. Why?

Mostly likely, it's because we're trying to solve spiritual problems with physical answers. We're working against ourselves and moving farther away from the solutions that we seek.

You've probably seen the poster of the little kitten that sees himself in the mirror as a fearsome lion. Like his, our self-image frames our perception of our personal power.

How do you see yourself? Whatever you perceive yourself to be—whether a fearful kitten or a ferocious lion—influences your beliefs. Your beliefs then guide your behavior, particularly how you treat others. The way you treat others today dictates how you will be treated tomorrow.

Simply put, mastery over the Law of Attraction—which also has been called the Law of Sowing and Reaping, and the Law of Compensation or Reciprocity—depends upon three interdependent factors, in this order: Your self image, which is influenced by others' perceptions of you; your beliefs, which are influenced by your self-image; and your actions, which are influenced by your beliefs.

These factors are inextricably connected. More important, they are the magnets that draw every experience into your life, so they deserve your immediate attention.

Envision your life as a circle. At the top: Your self-image. Everything starts with You and circles back to You. Your perception of who you are goes into the world and attracts experiences and people into your life that are drawn to that image of you. If your self-perception is incorrect or limited, you risk attracting things that you may not desire. Unfortunately, this is the case for most of us.

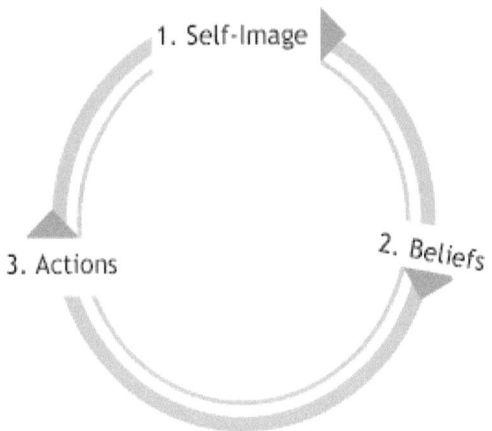

We're eager to end this vicious cycle and regain control of our lives, aren't we? That's why we readily embrace any solutions that appear to help us clear this hurdle.

Some well-meaning folks have told us about spiritual laws that basically guarantee our success in overcoming this problem. Lately, the one cited most frequently is the spiritual Law of Attraction, and we were given a process for activating it.

We were told that we must think more positively about what we wanted. *Heck, that was easy!* The next step, they suggested, was to vividly visualize our desired outcomes. *We loved every detail at first sight!* Then we were instructed to step it up a notch and add some emotion. They said that whatever we desire vibrates at a high frequency, and we needed to hum right along with it—actually feel the excitement of owning that house or car, and having that great job or perfect mate. *We could hardly wait to take that joyride!*

A lot of attention has been paid to those who have applied this law and have successfully attracted what they desired—or believed that they did. Millions more, however, followed each step and received nothing: No house, no car, no new job, no mate, no improvements in their health or relationships. In some cases, situations actually worsened.

If it's a law, shouldn't everyone have the same results? Is the Law of Attraction just hocus pocus? Or worse, is it bogus?

Neither, actually. Like all laws, the Law of Attraction works the same way 100% of the time. It worked for you, too. You might not have been aware of it because of your misperceptions of who you are and misunderstanding of who was asking for the goods. After you have a better understanding of who you are, you'll discover that you will receive precisely what you asked for. You always do.

I suspect that you were in such a rush to change your conditions that when you spotted a huge crowd running out of a bookstore like there was no tomorrow, you grabbed your jogging shoes and joined the pack.

Let me guess: you didn't train on a regular basis before the big race, did you? Didn't do one warm-up exercise, right?

I'm going to go out on a limb here and say that you probably didn't stretch before running, either; yet, you expected fantastic tangible results. Don't beat yourself up. Most of the runners thought it was a sprint, too.

Count me among them; I've been there. The lesson I learned from it is this: *Know who you are before deciding what you want.*

Here's why that matters: Let's say that I'm attending a prosperity or Law of Attraction seminar and the facilitator says, "Tell us your name and what you want. Remember, everything already exists in spirit, so paint a word picture, as if you already have it."

I might say, "I'm Pat, and I just returned home in my newest S-Class Mercedes—this one's black *(I'd giggle)*. I've done so much shopping on the Mag Mile that my driver had to call the housekeeper and cook to help him unload the car. They're getting my luggage now. I'm running late for my flight, and my sweetie is expecting me at our estate on the French Riviera early in the morning. He says he has a wonderful surprise for me!"

I'd clasp my hands over my heart and squeal with delight, as an admiring cheer would ripple through the room, "Aim high! Claim it, Girl! You *GO!*"

The young lady sitting next to me would then crank up her desire meter and say: "I'm Mickey, and our chauffeur has just driven one of our Bentleys onto the access road to the mountaintop estate on our private island, where my soul mate and I pay no taxes on our $5 billion annual income. We're arriving not a minute too soon, because I'm starved! Thank goodness, Cook will have a late lunch ready.

"It's been a hectic but exhilarating day. I was on my feet all morning, volunteering at the homeless shelter. Then I had to do a bit of back-to-school shopping for our adorable, brilliant, well-behaved son and daughter, who speak four languages and are prodigies on three musical instruments.

"We also have two champion show dogs and a filly who is a Derby contender. Everyone in our family enjoys optimum health, has a perfectly proportioned body, pearly white, absolutely straight teeth and gorgeous hair."

With a triumphant "Now, top that!" glance around the room, she sits. And so it goes, each person believing he or she is using the law to create a life of prosperity without limits.

Ironically, most Law of Attraction and "Create the Life You Want" coaching is predicated on two limiting assumptions: First, we are merely physical bodies, "meat suits," as philosopher James Arthur Ray calls humans; and second, our primary mission in life is to have anything we want in this physical world.

Let me be clear: I have nothing against "meat suits" or prosperity, for that matter. I like a great body and luxurious stuff as much as the next person; but how far can we go with that, really?

We are told that everything we desire already exists in the spiritual world, and we have the power to attract it onto the physical plane. In theory, a warehouse full of cool stainless steel refrigerators with TVs in the doors is beyond the physical plane. If we unleash the law, each of us can have one.

Are our mortal brains, our thinking faculties, really equipped to reach outside of the physical world, grab the high-vibrating goods and manifest them into physical form? That's something to think about. I'm confident our brainwaves can handle that task.

And think about this, too: If you're working with a spiritual law, but perceive yourself to be merely a physical body, what is the likelihood that you can direct your brain to communicate or vibrate at the same frequency as the nonphysical world?

Many of us have forgotten our elementary-school science classes. That's where we first learned some critical things about the physical world. For example, we discovered that everything in the Universe is comprised of matter and energy—constantly moving and vibrating atoms and molecules. This book, your body, a glass of water, a refrigerator, an office building, a car and even sound are merely vibrating atoms and molecules. None is solid matter.

What relevance does that have to the Law of Attraction? A lot, actually; it's going to help you remember how the law is activated so that you can effectively and consistently manifest your soul's desire rather than getting the spotty results most have experienced since the Law of Attraction frenzy began. Want to squeeze back into your fourth-grade seat now?

Remember when your teacher revealed that water has three forms: ice, water and steam? Teacher said that when water is exposed to temperatures below 0° centigrade, it freezes, and it becomes solid. Above that temperature, it's liquid—until the temperature exceeds 100° cx entigrade. At that point, the water becomes steam, which is often invisible. Solid, liquid or gas, dry or wet, hot or cold, visible or invisible, it is all the same thing: water. Hold that thought.

Early in our learning experience, we also were introduced to a genius quantum physicist named Albert Einstein, who elevated humans' understanding of matter to another level. Einstein said, "Mass and energy are both but different manifestations of the same thing—a somewhat unfamiliar conception for the average mind."

Einstein proved that physical matter and energy aren't distinct, they're equivalent. He expressed it in the now-famous equation $E=mc^2$.

In a nutshell, Einstein taught us that objects that appear to be solid really aren't. They are actually atoms and molecules vibrating at such a slow rate that we can see them with the physical eye. Buildings, boats and even our bodies are really energy vibrating so slowly that they make lethargy look like it's moving at the speed of light. But regardless of the speed at which it moves, all matter is energy. It's not solid.

What does that mean to you, O Humble Walking Magnet? I'll let you tell me.

What is Energy, Einstein?

Is it solid?	Yes	No
Can it be created or destroyed?	Yes	No
Is it a physical body?	Yes	No
Is it limited to space and time?	Yes	No
Can it move in and out of a form such as a mortal body?	Yes	No
Was there a time when it never existed?	Yes	No
Is there a time when it never will exist?	Yes	No

Then What is Matter?

Is it solid?	Yes	No
Can it be created or destroyed?	Yes	No
Is it a physical body?	Yes	No
Is it limited to space and time?	Yes	No
Can it move in and out of a form such as a mortal body?	Yes	No
Was there a time when it never existed?	Yes	No
Is there a time when it never will exist?	Yes	No

You're a genius, so I don't have to tell you that the answer to all of these questions is no. And from first-semester algebra, you probably also know the answer to this question:

If a = b and b = c, then a = ___?

Let's look at it another way: If your body is matter and matter is energy, what are you? Are you a body that has a finite life span or the indestructible energy that gives your body life?

If you are energy, and energy moves into, through and out of a physical form, do you? If there was never a time when energy didn't exist, was there ever a time when you didn't exist? If there will never be a time when energy doesn't exist, will there ever be a time when you don't exist?

Failing to make the distinction between physical life and the infinite energy that is Life itself can result in undesired and limited consequences. For example, if you believe that you are a visible physical being with a temporary life, you will have different desires and limit yourself to creating physical things.

On the other hand, if you believe that you are a spark of the infinite, immortal energy that is Life itself you will want to create on a higher, infinite level. You are less likely to focus on attracting physical things into your life. Your desires will be a lot more expansive, your creations will be more powerful and your prosperity will ultimately be greater than if you limited yourself to attracting visible, slow moving molecules in the physical world.

Law of Attraction enthusiasts tell us that we can manifest anything we desire by making it our dominant thought. Only on Earth would we entrust a three-pound brain to do such heavy lifting! Quite possibly, they are urging us to send a plumber to do an electrician's job. That could explain why any success we enjoy in manifesting our desires is more coincidental than consistent—individual rather than collective, exceptions, not common occurrences.

If we continue to do what we're doing, we're going to keep sprinting down that well-worn path to Nowhere—nowhere evolutionary, anyway. Once you understand who and what you really are, you might discover that Life itself is an open book and that absolutely no secrets have been kept from you.

As you grow in self-awareness, as you discover just how great and powerful you really are, you will likely begin to use that power more consistently and effectively. You will be a natural magnet for physical objects and beings that are greater blessings to you than your mortal brain could have imagined.

Your perception and understanding of yourself as mortal or immortal play a significant role in determining what you desire, as well as what kind of experiences you will have in life.

What is your self-image? If you're not sure, take look at the characteristics of those with mortal and immortal self-images and determine which one describes you:

<u>**MORTALS**</u>	<u>**IMMORTALS**</u>
Try to manipulate the law to work for them.	*Effortlessly work with the law, following its lead.*
Are fearful; they hope that the law will work.	*Are powerful; they know that it works unfailingly.*
Create from their brains and limit their desires to what they can see.	*Create from the Divine energy within them, desiring what has never been seen.*

If you could create anything in the Universe, would you spend time creating slowly moving molecules in the physical world, or would you create something that more genuinely reflected the pure energy within your eternal power center?

Who are you?

Close your eyes and look within your physical costume. Ask, "Who am I?"

Just be still and wait for the response. At some point, you might see a small circle of brilliant light vibrating in the center of your body. Notice that as you acknowledge its presence, the light seems to glow more brightly.

You might feel a warm, tingling sensation in the center of your physical body or you might instinctively take a deep breath, as if inhaling the Light into every atom of your being. Perhaps you sigh, feeling deeply relaxed. Maybe you want to linger in the glow of the Light because it feels as if it is protecting you from the fears and insecurities of the physical world.

Maybe you saw and felt nothing at all. Don't be concerned. Your Light simply might be on the energy-saving setting because it's been dormant for so many decades. The good news is that the Light didn't burn out; and it can glow brightly again, whenever you desire.

That's true for all of us. We can make a conscious decision to let our Light guide our choices and our actions, or we can go it alone without acknowledging or leveraging its power. Our free will grants us this right; but each choice we make has a natural—not negative or positive—consequence.

Our beliefs about ourselves, others and God write the requisitions for the experiences that return to us through the spiritual Law of Attraction. We can choose to remember that and consciously receive joy, or we can continue to forget and unconsciously attract pain. The Law works with or without our awareness or intentional participation.

Life was not intended to be difficult or cause unhappiness, and was not meant to be unfair. Only a sadist would create a world such as that. Do we believe that God would do something so diabolical and inhumane? You might be surprised by your true beliefs.

Next, we'll look at what you believe about yourself, God and others—and the role that your beliefs play in determining what the spiritual Law of Attraction delivers to you, day in and day out.

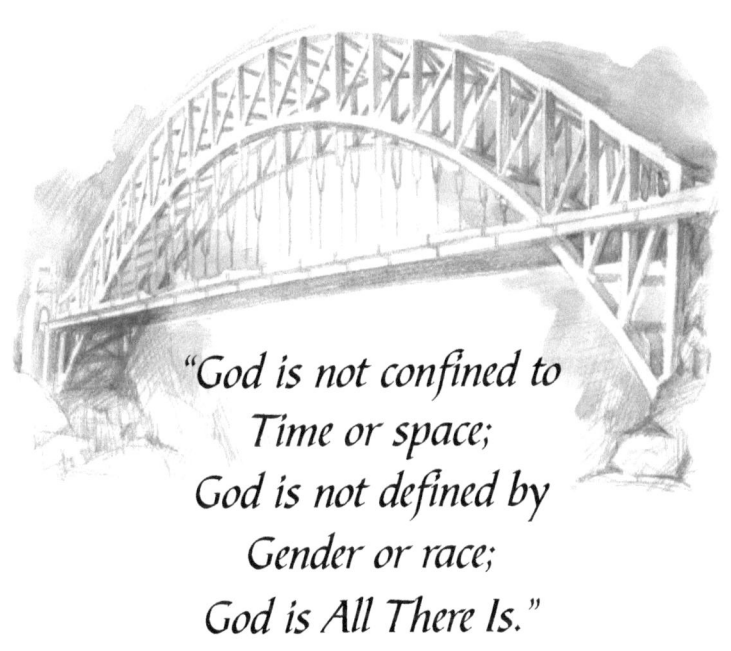

"God is not confined to
Time or space;
God is not defined by
Gender or race;
God is All There Is."

Loud Mouth in the Balcony
www.balcony-loudmouth.com

Secret #2

Understand Your Beliefs — and Their Implications

It's probably no coincidence that the word "manipulate" begins with "man." I'm not saying that manipulative behavior is limited to a certain gender—or culture, race or nationality, for that matter. It's just that because it's such a pervasive human characteristic, I wouldn't be surprised if it's a strand in our DNA—probably protruding like a cowlick, poised to block another strand from doing its thing.

As humans, we love to manipulate things, and really get a kick out of controlling others: where and how they live, what they wear, what they own, whom they love and marry, what they say—and to whom. Some even like to control what we believe about God. In fact, they seem to care less about whether we believe in God than *what* we believe about God.

Let's face it: All of us, including atheists, have beliefs about God, and those beliefs indirectly impact the Law of Attraction—or Reciprocity or Reaping and Sowing—whatever name we want to call this spiritual law. How is that possible?

The Law of Attraction works 24/7, responding directly to every action and reaction, constantly returning to us what we've given, doing to us what we've done. If we drew a line from our actions backward to their genesis, that line would go directly to our beliefs: what we believe about ourselves, others and, perhaps most important, what we believe about God:

> ❃ Do we believe that God is patient or demanding, loving or judgmental, vengeful or forgiving?

> ❃ Do we believe that God brings Light into the room or casts a scary shadow?

> ❃ Do we believe that some souls are not worthy of God's time and presence, or does our God embrace all prodigal children?

It's important to understand what we believe about God because our beliefs impact the way we treat others and subsequently dictate the way we will be treated. It's the law, and that's no secret.

We must look closely at our beliefs to determine if they are valid, then make any necessary adjustments so that what returns to us are things we don't regret. Otherwise, we run the risk of having unrealistic expectations of the Law when it completes its cycle from Self to Self—and those refrigerators with built-in TVs will never manifest in our kitchens.

Many teachers of what I call the Partial Law of Attraction assert that we can manipulate the law with our brains. They've told us that we can repeat mantras, maintain positive thoughts, become emotional and, as a result, create spectacular things.

We might be fooled, but the law is not. It is going to work the same way, no matter what we say, think, feel or visualize.

How many of us have had great relationships or jobs and never thought that they'd end? How many of us were proved wrong, despite our positive thinking? How many of us have made detailed plans, visualized our success, yet we failed? If everything had unfolded as planned, would we have attributed it to the Law of Attraction?

Many enthusiasts make that claim because they don't understand the law. I'm reminded of an executive who saw a gadget in a catalog and told a friend that he'd like to have one. Later that day, he spotted a package in his office, a birthday gift from his assistant. Inside was the same gadget he'd just said that he wanted. It had been in his office for months. But because he hadn't seen it there until after he mentioned it, he was absolutely convinced that he'd manifested it through the powerful Law of Attraction.

Never mind that the unopened package probably had caught his assistant's eye every time she walked into his office. Can you imagine how she felt, knowing he'd ignored it?

Just for the record: Because the Law of Attraction reportedly materializes things from the invisible spiritual realm into the visible physical realm, that doesn't mean that it causes us to suddenly see things that were already in front of our faces. Sorry.

What about claims that we can activate the law by doing, feeling and saying something? Actually, the law isn't waiting for our call, our thought or our emotions. It is working, even when we're not actively or consciously working it. The law ceaselessly responds to our state of being and the actions that we take while we're in that state. Many of our actions are based on our conscious and unconscious beliefs.

Since our beliefs have so much influence in our lives and might be separating us from the joyful people, experiences and even the material things we desire, we might benefit from giving more thought to what we believe and why we believe it. Our beliefs have given the illusion that Life is quite complicated and grossly unfair. As a result, these beliefs have attracted tremendous pain and unhappiness.

Are you curious enough to closely examine your beliefs and what they may be attracting? Are you ready to connect the dots?

If I took a poll, most would say that they believe that children who feel unloved tend to exhibit unlovable, negative and destructive behavior. It's interesting then that many of us subscribe to the belief that humans are not worthy of being in God's sight; we are not loved unconditionally and must do or say something to win God's love. How does that make us feel? How does it make us act?

Similarly, most of us believe that children who are treated unfairly, especially by a parent, have difficulty trusting others. At the same time, we also believe that God blames us for the naïve error made thousands of years ago by the first primitive beings that our Heavenly Father created.

It's no doubt that Adam and Eve were more childlike than cavemen. They couldn't have been logical analytic thinkers. God certainly knew that. Was it fair to severely punish these two pre-Neanderthal creatures, who were born as adults but acted like mischievous children, by banishing them from the only home they knew?

Since childhood, we have believed that God has refused to unconditionally forgive any human since that prehistoric error. And we wonder why we don't trust God to help us through life's storms. Maybe it's because, deep down, we believe that God is unfair.

Have we stopped to consider how mistrust in the Invisible might block our ability to make a spiritual law to work for us? Is there a connection between our belief that God has an angry, unforgiving nature and our own angry, unforgiving responses to others' errors?

Ironically, most who believe that God severely punishes also believe that God is Love. The implication here is that Divine Love responds to error with brutal punishment rather than unconditional forgiveness, and that Divine Love unfairly holds others accountable for someone else's disobedience.

Is that what we really believe? It's important to understand what we believe and what our beliefs mean. It's just as important to be consistent. For example, if we believe that it is divinely fair for all humans to be held personally accountable for Adam and Eve's disobedience, why don't we turn ourselves in to authorities when a relative, friend, neighbor, co-worker or resident of our city, state or country is convicted of a crime?

The truth is that we really don't believe that one person should be accused or punished for another's misdeed. Why do we believe that God does that?

If parents punish their kids severely, kick them out of the house or tell them that they're unworthy to be in the same room, most of us would be compelled to call the authorities. There are laws against that kind of abuse. Why do we believe God did anything of the sort?

If we believe that live sacrifices are satanic, why do we believe that God has ever demanded live sacrifices as penance for human error? If we believe that genocide is evil, why do we believe that God murdered every human being, but a few, and a small menagerie—and has threatened to do it again?

Are these really our beliefs, or have we embraced others' beliefs without questions?

Great minds think when they choose to, and many of us choose not. For example, millions of great minds not only believe that God behaves like a heartless mass murderer, they believe that God's Great Flood victims disappeared into thin air. *Poof! Gone!* No remains, and no one has questioned where they went.

I'm not sure many have even thought about that when they repeat this hurt-filled story as if it is a chapter in human history. Some are even outraged if anyone questions its veracity. The fact that it's in the Bible is a greater testament to its truth than the fact that it portrays God as a genocidal despot.

They insist that God was so furious with humans' wickedness that, forgetting He was infallible, He claimed to have made a mistake by creating them. (Gen 6:6). Despite His omniscience, He could think of only one way to correct it: "Destroy all flesh, wherein is the breath of life, from under heaven; and everything that is in the earth shall die." (Gen 6:17)

God determined that there was only one virtuous human on earth, 600-year-old Noah, and instructed this very old man to build a vessel longer than a football field and about three stories tall, and to board his family and a variety of ferocious and docile animals to spare them from God's first genocidal act.

In the two pages that relate this unique planet-soaked flood, the text offers a contradictory tally of the actual number of wild beasts and creepy crawly things—the planet's entire food chain—that arrived on schedule, formed an orderly queue and meekly walked from freedom and fresh air into the darkness of the cavernous ark through its only door.

According to the text, there were as many as 14 of every species on earth. It does not mention how those who lived many kilometers or continents away from Noah's neighborhood actually found the ark, but they coexisted in the dark on this primitively constructed vessel.

The rain was "upon the earth" for seven days. (Gen 7:10) It rained for 40 days. (Gen 7:12) I mean 150 days. (Gen 7:24) No, make that seven months. (Gen 8:4)

Even if we fail to see those glaring discrepancies, what's missing is even more troublesome. Think, great minds. Yes! There's no mention of the endless waterscape of bloated bodies—wicked infants, children, teens, adults and animals—and their awful stench, which must have surrounded the ark and floated alongside it, with the current.

The good news is that God had instructed Noah to build only one window on the ark, so the smell of the rotting bodies wasn't rushing in on all sides of the vessel. The bad news is that the ark had only one window, so the smell of the wild animals on board—both dead and alive (and defecating)—couldn't escape, either.

It seems to me that the human and other creatures on the boat were more severely punished than the flood victims, whose deaths were relatively swift. The survivors, on the other hand, disembarked from the torturous ride, parched, hungry, sleep deprived, weak and aching, only to discover that none of the water was potable; the dead bodies had contaminated it. Every plant and tree was root-rotted, so they bore no food. What could the survivors eat? I can imagine that Noah and his famished sons eyed the animals, and the famished animals eyed them.

We're to believe that humans who were hundreds of years old survived this torture! Maybe this is why Noah later became a drunk.

Stories such as this portray God as a sadist who even tortures good people. That's a bit problematic for those of us who believe that God is Love. Would Love do that?

If we believe these stories, as millions do, solving problems by mistreating, torturing or killing people becomes the Word of God, which might explain some of the violent actions and reactions we see in today's headlines.

Some say that only those who misinterpret the Bible would conclude that it promotes violence, so out of curiosity, I searched *The New Strong's Expanded Exhaustive Concordance of the Bible* (Thomas Nelson Publishers, 2001) for the words "death," "kill(ed)," "slaughter," "slay," and "smite." I encountered no fewer than 363 references to or commands for deadly force. The phrase repeated most often was the command, *"...shall be put to death."*

What offenses were cited as warranting the death penalty? It varied from murder (Num 35:16-18) to blaspheming (Lev 24:16) and adultery (Lev 20:10) to being a stranger who walked by a temple (Num 1:51). Kidnapping and selling a person are also punishable by death. Note to teens: so is cursing at or hitting one's parent (Lev 21:15-17).

If this is the word of the unchanging God, millions today are in mortal danger because they work on Saturdays: "...[O]n the seventh day there shall be to you an holy day, a sabbath of rest to the LORD: whosoever doeth work therein *shall be put to death."* (Ex 35:2).

In some cases, the mandate to respond violently to error describes precisely how the erring person should be put to death: "...[T]he people of the land shall stone him with stones." (Lev 20:2)

Why do we defend stories that portray God as behaving less than divine? Does Divine Love solve problems with murder?

I am not saying that there is no Truth in the Bible; however, everything in the Bible couldn't possibly be true. If it was the Word of God, wouldn't it be?

I'm not advocating that you believe one thing or another, only that you understand what you believe and understand the implications of your beliefs because they influence your behavior. Your beliefs can make you hurt others—and attract pain, in response.

Humans have always been in a quandry about why certain things occur. Many ancient stories reveal how they resolved Life's mysteries. Often, they attempted to control as many circumstances as possible, and as many people who permitted.

Ancient people weren't sophisticated, but they weren't stupid, either. There were aspects of the Earth experience that they didn't like and couldn't explain, such as natural disasters. They concluded that someone extremely forceful and quite fearsome was causing these catastrophic conditions. They were certain that someone was out there, over there, up there, somewhere. They couldn't see who it was, which terrified them even more.

They suspected that the object of their fear was a gigantic god beyond the clouds. He occasionally made the skies very dark and dangerous. There was roaring wind and pelting rain. He flashed dangerous bolts of light and bellowed frightening rumbling noises. The rumbling would crescendo then fade, as though he was walking across the heavens, moving a great distance with each step.

They concluded that he was furious with humans, because the storms were frequently destructive and sometimes deadly to those below. They wanted his life-giving rain, but not the hurricanes, tornadoes or thunderstorms.

In the ancient world, this god was declared the most powerful of all. The Greeks called him Zeus; to the Romans, he was Jupiter. To worshippers, he was "Father," the undisputed master of the Universe.

The ancient Greeks and Romans believed that Zeus/Jupiter ruled the skies and thunder. Their artwork and statues frequently portrayed him as an enormous man with a bolt of lightning in his hand.

Despite his obvious superiority, Zeus's life story was similar to those of pagan gods who reigned several millennia before and after him. According to myth, ancient gods always demanded unfaltering worship and obedience, and painful, sometimes, deadly sacrifice. They commonly committed crimes against humanity, such as genocide and filicide, in fits of anger, jealousy or revenge.

The myth of Hephaestus, which I recently saw performed as an intricate, breathtaking and wildly entertaining circus act, typifies the genre: Hephaestus, the god of fire, was born lame. According to legend, his mother, the goddess Hera (wife of Zeus), threw her imperfect son from the top of Mount Olympus. He fell through the atmosphere for nine days and was rescued by nymphs. He later avenged his mother's failed filicide attempt by creating a beautiful chariot for her and imprisoning her in it. She won her release by presenting him with a live offering: the beautiful Aphrodite.

Ancient myths abound of gods who did despicable things. Many raped human virgins and produced earthly sons who later ruled their subjects by divine right. Worshippers accepted these myths and expected all of their gods to fit into this mold.

Myths are stories, not history. They stir the imagination. Picture Zeus indiscriminately lobbing lightning bolts from the heavens whenever he tired of humans' misbehavior. We can imagine that the first rumble of thunder probably made ancient Greeks tremble in their togas, wondering which heathen had riled mighty Zeus. They caucused to discuss ways to control his raging storms—after all, their very lives depended on it.

They tried one solution after another to appease the "Father" and quell his anger. They built temples. They created rituals of worship and praise. They even sacrificed innocent animals and offered them to "The Man Upstairs."

What extraordinary gesture could they make to garner Zeus's favor *(and prevent the violent storms, thank you very much)?* Absolutely nothing seemed to work. The lightning and thunder always seemed to return, no matter what they did or how extreme their sacrifices. Nothing appeared to please Zeus.

When he was in a good mood, the sun would shine or light rain would fall. When he was full of wrath, he would open the skies with deadly force. If it came from the heavens, Zeus did it; the ancient Greeks believed it, and that's all there was to it. This is fascinating stuff, and it reveals why we should read more than one ancient book to understand the genesis and revelations of human belief. We'd discover some surprising parallels between ancient myth and modern religion.

For example, after the waters receded from the Great Flood, Noah built an altar, took every clean beast and fowl and burned them as offerings to God. (Gen 8:21) For this they survived that horrible ride in the ark? The story claims that God was so pleased by the "sweet savour" of the burning meat that wafted millions of miles through the atmosphere that He promised never to destroy the earth again because, after all, "the imagination of man's heart *is* evil from his youth." (Gen 8:21) In other words, we can't help ourselves. God knew that before committing genocide, right?

I'm not mocking these fanciful stories. They have great value. They provide a window into the minds and culture of ancient peoples. That's a treasure, when viewed in context.

Modern theologians and Biblical scholars have dramatically provided that context and improved the religious literacy of the masses. They have lifted the curtain on the history of human belief—what we believe and why—in easy-to-read works such as *A Short History of Myth* and *A History of God* by former Roman Catholic nun Karen Armstrong, Professor Marcus J. Borg's *Reading the Bible Again for the First Time,* Kenneth C. Davis's *Don't Know Much About the Bible,* Biblical scholar Bart D. Ehrman's *Misquoting Jesus: The Story Behind*

Who Changed the Bible and Why and *Who Wrote the Bible?* by Hebrew Bible Professor Richard Elliott Friedman. Retired Episcopalian Bishop John Shelby Spong, who does not believe that the Bible is the word of God, has stirred considerable controversy with his books, including *Rescuing the Bible from Fundamentalism* and *The Sins of Scripture*, as has Dan Brown's fictional bestseller *The DaVinci Code*. These books and others have provided jaw-dropping insights into the mythical origins of current religious beliefs and actual events. I encourage you to read them.

Because of the popularity of these authors' works, millions of laypeople now know what divinity students have known for ages: At the first ecumenical council of Christian bishops, convened by Roman Emperor Constantine in 325A.D. at Nicea (now in Turkey), nearly 300 men examined conflicting texts about Jesus and agreed on one Christian doctrine. In effect, that group of men decided what books would be included in the Bible and what Christians would believe from that point on.

For 1,114 years, Christians relied on church leaders to tell them what to believe. Bibles were handwritten, rare and inaccessible to the masses. This gave the clergy tremendous authority over their flocks and positioned them as possessing greater knowledge and having a closer relationship with God. Followers were expected to believe every word and were threatened with unpleasant consequences if they didn't.

Bibles have been in great supply for the past 500 years, but most of us still rely on others to read it for us. Some even read it and cannot to see glaring contradictions in facts and figures or do not detect the implications of what the text is saying about God.

As Shakespeare said, "Even the devil can cite scripture for his purpose." Some say Shakespeare is the writer of the King James version, which begs another question: Why are there "versions" of God's word? And why do we avoid certain portions of the text, quoting only those passages that we're comfortable with? If it's all true, we should be able to randomly open any page and resonate with its message.

I have never heard anyone read this verse from Ezra (6:11) aloud: "...[W]hosoever shall alter this word, let timber be pulled down from his house, and being set up, let him be hanged thereon..." Sounds like a lynching to me.

When we read with our "this is the truth, the whole truth and nothing but the truth" lenses, we see one thing. When we wear "God is good all the time and all the time, God is good" lenses, we see something else. For example, it's easier to detect that The Great Flood is not one story, it's a combination of four different versions of an ancient myth. That's why the facts and head count changes from one sentence to another. Different tribes had different stories. They wove them together—and not seamlessly: In Gen 7:9-10, Noah gets on the boat with one quantity of animals; it rains for seven days. In Gen 7:12, it rains for 40 days and nights and in the next verse, Noah and the animals inexplicably get on the boat.

    I could be wrong, but God's word would be indisputably inerrant and consistent. How many have noticed that the Bible claims that Jesus was born in different locations during different years or that he died on different days? Where does it say that he was born on December 25? What does ancient mythology tell us about that date?

    December 25, four days after the winter solstice, ancient peoples could detect with naked eyes that the sun appeared higher in the sky. Its warmth would last a bit longer with each passing day. It signaled a new beginning, new life; and it was cause for great celebration. And what a celebration—complete with gift giving and candle lighting.

For thousands of years, many of the most revered gods in the ancient world were said to have been born on December 25. All were humans, conceived of a virgin mother who had been impregnated by a great pagan god.

It's more than conjecture that Christian leaders at the Council of Nicea appropriated both the birthday and the biographies of these gods to convert the pagan masses to Christianity.

In one of the strongest ironies of human history, those who didn't accept the Prince of Peace's biography were brutally killed. Church leaders believed that God would have done the same. Even today, what defines someone as a Christian is whether that person believes Jesus's birth and death narratives, not whether he or she embodies his teachings of love, forgiveness and Oneness with God.

Thousands of years ago, an astute theorist named Xenophanes, a predecessor of the Greek philosopher Socrates, observed that humans have a knack for creating gods in their own image. The evidence is clear: Drawings of Egyptians' gods portrayed them as flat-nosed and dark, like the Egyptians. Thracians' gods were blue-eyed redheads, like the Thracians. The rest of their bodies also resembled humans'.

Xenophanes opined that if animals could draw, horses probably would create gods that looked like horses and oxen would create gods that looked like oxen.

In addition to creating a god who looks like humans, we appear to have created one who, like Zeus, acts more inhumane than divine. Oddly enough, we seem to be unaware of what we've actually created. For example...

Most of us believe that:

1) God is a male being;

2) He once walked in the Garden of Eden;

3) One day He left the garden; and

4) When He returned, He couldn't find Adam and Eve because they were hiding.

What do these beliefs mean?

1) Like humans, God has gender—*so God is not spirit;*

2) Like humans, God has a physical body—*so God is not infinite;*

3) Like humans, God can be in only one place at a time—*so God is not omnipresent;* and

4) Like humans, God doesn't know everything—*so God is not omniscient.*

It's the 21st century, and we are still following the lead of primitive people who were trying to understand the natural disasters in their flat little world. Back then, Earth was the center of the Universe, and the sun they worshipped revolved around it. They were as certain of that as they were that the tyrannical lightning-zapper, Zeus, was watching them from the other side of the clouds.

The ancients had access to few data resources. Their myths and beliefs reflected what they knew about the world—and what they didn't know. They knew nothing of astronomy, geography, climatology, meteorology or genetics. They didn't know how large the world was. My goodness, they didn't even know the planet was round! If it was raining where they were, they believed that it was raining throughout world. They couldn't view satellite-transmitted pictures of weather conditions, so they had no way of knowing that it never rains everywhere at the same time.

Today, despite our access to instruments and data that clearly refute the ancients' view of reality, many of us still hold onto our errant beliefs about what God is and what God does. Those beliefs still motivate our punitive behavior and influence what returns to us through the Law of Attraction.

Do our beliefs exalt or diminish God? We probably haven't taken time to think about that. Until now, we had no idea how much our beliefs influence our behavior, either. Let's get an idea by connecting a few more dots:

- If we believe that God punishes, are we more / less likely to do the same?

- If we believe that God forgives under certain conditions, are we more / less likely to withhold forgiveness until someone meets our conditions?

- If we believe that God "blesses" or "favors" some humans over others, are we more / less likely to do the same?

- If we believe that God promotes violence as a solution to disagreements, are we more / less likely to do the same?

- If we believe that God favors our religion, are we more / less likely to feel that other faiths are inferior or unacceptable?

- If we believe that God is controlling, punitive and judgmental, are we more / less likely to mimic that behavior?

- If we believe that God hates same sex relationships, are we more / less likely to hate them?

Want to try a few more?

🌠 Someone who says, "Do as I say, not as I do!" is admirable / hypocritical.

🌠 Someone who tortures or kills those who won't follow orders is dictatorial / democratic.

🌠 Someone who kicks a child out of the house because she was disobedient is heartless / exemplary.

🌠 Someone who blames or punishes one person for a crime someone else committed is fair / unjust.

🌠 A parent who knowingly leaves children in the care and control of someone known to be abusive would be called inhumane / wise.

Look at the words you've circled. Now you know how you really feel about acts that God reportedly has confessed to committing. Is that confession credible—or do you believe it because it has been declared scripture?

Again, I am not suggesting what you should believe. The world doesn't need a "Gospel According to Pat," as a lovely nun friend joked. I am, however, suggesting that you understand what your beliefs really mean.

Do your beliefs portray God as divine or demonic? Does the God you believe in adhere to a lower standard of conduct than one that you deem acceptable for humans?

If you want the Law of Attraction to manifest positively in your life, you must understand that your beliefs about yourself and about God directly influence the way you treat others. And, as you'll see in the next chapter, how you treat others determines whether you consciously attract what you desire or unconsciously attract what you deserve.

A contemporary philosopher of note summed up this Challenge of the Ages quite profoundly when he said, "When you believe in things you don't understand, then you suffer."

Thanks for that insight, Stevie. It's just one more reason to call you a "wonder."

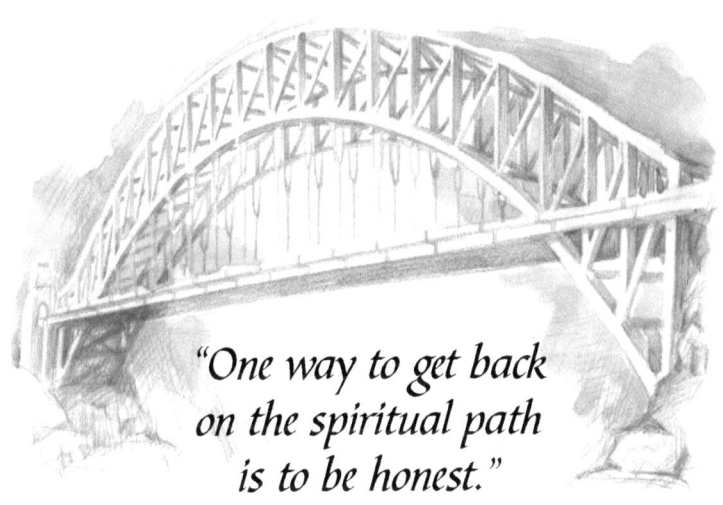

"One way to get back on the spiritual path is to be honest."

John-Roger

Loving Each Day- Reflections on the Spirit Within -- John-Roger, DSS
Copyright (c) 1989, 2000 Peace Theological Seminary & College of Philosophy
Mandeville Press, ISBN: 978-0-914829-26-3
Mandeville Press, 3500 West Adams Blvd., Los Angeles, CA 90018
www.mandevillepress.org

Secret #3

Act as if Life Is Round

I was having lunch with a friend when she said the most amazing thing. At the time, she was going through a contentious divorce, following years of disrespect, betrayal and even physical abuse by her husband and children.

When I expressed empathy with her situation, she raised an eyebrow. "It's OK, life is round," she said, grinning.

My friend's overall peacefulness in that moment was remarkable. I was sure that I would've been ready to fight if anyone had treated me so horribly.

Recalling that incident now, I realize that my reaction revealed two things about me: Number one, I harbored religious prejudices. I hadn't expected a Jewish woman to say something so, uh, Christlike. There, I said it—but don't ask me to explain it. After all, the man we know as Jesus was a Jew. I knew that. Number two, I discovered that I had been giving lip service to principles that this woman was actually practicing in her daily life.

I teach four basic principles in my Drama Queen Workshops.™ The very first principle is "Life is always FAIR"—or, as my friend phrased it, "Life is ROUND." The message of this principle is simple and familiar: What goes around comes around, so it is always in our best interest to treat every situation, every error and every person the way we'd want to be treated. That's why the rule is golden.

If others violate this principle, the natural consequences of their actions will even the score; we don't have to. We can trust that and trust God.

It's only now, as I recall that lunch conversation, that I realize I had been teaching that lesson from my intellect rather than from my heart. If I had I been in her shoes, I surely would have tried to personally even the score.

Of course, that day at lunch, I didn't have that insight or see the irony—OK, the hypocrisy—in my public words versus my private thoughts. It didn't occur to the human part of me that I lacked integrity.

The eternal part of me, however, was painfully aware. And, in the months that followed, my soul attracted a series of opportunities for me to practice what I preached.

Shortly after that lunch date, a well-known businessman wanted to hire my consulting services. He had an immediate crisis communications problem and long-term public relations needs. He was familiar with my work, but did not have my business card and didn't know the name of my company. A mutual business associate led him to me. One day, he dropped by my building. From the doorman's phone, he asked if we could meet later that week. I was absolutely stunned.

By the time we met, I had recovered from the initial shock. After reviewing my proposal and hourly rate, my prospective client decided that he wanted me to give undivided attention to his issues, and requested a one-year contract for full-time servicing of his account.

I had to pinch myself. Surely, God had sent this man. After all, he had miraculously appeared in my lobby, hadn't he?

I had only one concern: My prospective client frequently boasted that he prayed at five o'clock in the morning, attended not one but three church services on Sundays and he sinccerely believed in a "Do as I say, not as I do"

God who threatened to torture anyone who didn't love Him or do as commanded.

I hoped it wouldn't become a problem, but as long as he allowed me to believe that God was greater and acted a whole lot better than that, I was sure we'd get along. We shook hands, and I agreed to submit a contract.

Within the next few days, I wrapped up my outstanding projects and turned down an opportunity to bid on a more lucrative long-term contract. After all, I'd made a commitment to a guy who seriously needed help.

A week after my new client signed my contract—and I'd begun to work—his first months' retainer check returned, unpaid. I was furious!

When I marched to his building, he happened to be standing in the lobby. I didn't want to create a scene, so I headed to an elevator without saying a word. He wondered why I hadn't acknowledged him when I entered the building, so he followed me into the elevator.

Brave man. The moment the door closed, I let him have it, literally backing him into a corner. It didn't matter that he was three times my size; from the first floor to the 43rd, my finger was in his face as I ranted about integrity and trustworthiness.

My finger should have been in my own face. I'd seen a mound of evidence that my client was not an honorable man. After all, his alleged lack of integrity had created his crisis communications problem. It was also the reason his once-successful empire had collapsed.

He had portrayed himself as a man who had reformed. He was humble and repentant. He'd found God. He needed someone to fight his cause while he rebuilt his business and his life, and he'd heard that I enjoyed a challenge.

I had weighed his words carefully before reaching my decision: This Bible-totin', five-o'clock-in-the-mornin'-prayin', three-Sunday-services-attendin' Christian deserved a break. (And let's not forget that I was convinced that he had been divinely sent to my lobby.) But as I prepared to leave the elevator that day, the signals were both mixed and weak; I wasn't sure in which direction I should turn.

My client pleaded for me to keep the account. He swore that the returned check was a bank glitch, not an indication of financial problems. He even arranged for his bank to pay my monthly retainer by wire transfer, since I would no longer accept his checks.

Several months later, after he'd consistently transferred only a fraction of our agreed monthly retainer, my client (and I) finally admitted that he could not afford my services.

I kept thinking about the lucrative opportunity I had rejected within hours of agreeing to work for this man. And, of course, there was that gaping hole in my income that was getting deeper, every month that his retainer fell far short of my living expenses. Those thoughts held a few of my brain cells captive, too.

Relief seemed on the way the day my former client announced that he had a financially solvent business associate who needed a broad range of marketing communications services. He assured me his recommendation would give me an advantage over the others who were pitching the business.

I quickly assembled a talented team of professionals to partner with me, and spent a few sleepless nights developing our presentation. After reviewing and approving my slides, my former client arranged for us to present our proposal to his friend.

The company headquarters, the business owner and his staff were very impressive. I also liked the ethics expressed in the company's mission statement.

The owner had been in business more than 20 years and his enterprise was still growing. Landing a contract with this company would clearly be a phenomenal opportunity for my team.

After our first presentation, the owner was extremely pleased. At the end of the second presentation, he jumped up from his chair, absolutely delighted. We were his team of choice. Could we start the next day?

Was he kidding? Actually, I guess he was. Weeks later, our contract remained unsigned. Neither I nor my team members had accepted other work, thinking that we would launch this project at any moment.

After more than a month of ignoring my phone calls and correspondence, the owner called my office and announced that he would be ready to move forward within a week or so. Obviously, it was "or so." I never heard from the man again.

Maybe these two business associates guzzled from the same goblet of dubious integrity; I didn't have a clue. All I knew was that I was desperately clinging to a bowed-and-about-to-break financial limb, and if something didn't happen quick, fast and in a hurry, I was going to lose the roof over my head.

What most concerned me was that I was once again on the financial roller coaster that I'd ridden for nearly 20 years. I thought I had lowered the curtain on that drama. I wanted to create a story with a much happier ending. What lesson had I not learned?

My wonderful, caring friends were very supportive through this, yet another reversal of fortune. They prescribed several prosperity treatments and Law of Attraction remedies. More than a few times, it was suggested that I should "claim" what I wanted and get emotional, so that I could take charge and control my destiny. They recommended books and CDs; some loving souls even sent them to me.

I truly appreciated what my friends were trying to do. I knew that they sincerely wanted me to prosper. They'd heard about these tactics working for some folks, and they wanted to believe that they would work for me. I was not convinced. I had tried all these techniques years earlier, had followed the directions to the letter, and nothing had happened.

I've come to believe that a law is only a law if it works the same way for 100% of the people, 100% of the time. Laws of gravitation, motion, chemistry, thermodynamics, quantum mechanics, energy and gas don't produce different results for one person than they do for another. If thousands of fans release balloons in an arena, none of them is going to crash onto the field. If they let go of their hot dogs, none will fly toward the sky. The law works the same way for everyone.

Despite the Law of Attraction's apparently inconsistent results, my friends and I concurred that somewhere inside this material lay a grain of Truth. However, that wasn't enough for me—I wanted the whole truth. More than a paying client and financial solvency, I desired to connect with that Truth.

I also wasn't willing to entrust my finite physical self to run the show when my Infinite Self was much more competent. I wanted to try to align with God's will, not find new and wonderful ways to impose my will on God.

I probably could have chosen a less risky time to relinquish control of my life. After all, what if the ancient secrets had finally worked for me? But, as Einstein said, the definition of "insanity is doing the same thing over and over again, but expecting different results." I was flirting with a breakdown, but I wasn't insane.

I had done a considerable amount of spiritual homework for a mighty long time. I had grown tremendously through the process, but apparently not enough, if this was reoccurring. I wanted my breakthrough. In the interim, I was willing to settle for a break.

Miraculously, it appeared that one was on the way. After witnessing his friend jerk me around for a couple of months and still desperately in need of my services himself, my former client called with a life line. He knew that I wasn't the slightest bit entertained by his first performance, but he also knew that I needed to fill the gaping hole in my project grid with a client with both integrity and money in the bank. So he disguised himself as one.

The karma creatin' clown tried to dupe me into doing a massive project, knowing that he couldn't pay me! Despite all that time he'd spent with his minister, all the church services he'd attended every Sunday and all the Bible passages he'd read, this man hadn't stumbled across any of the 16 verses declaring that we reap what we sow. I know it pales when compared with the number of times "shall be put to death" appears, but still it's a significant number of mentions.

I thought about the hypocrisy of this man as I walked home from his office that chilly morning; in fact, I could think of nothing else. And, after a really good cry, I knew that I had to do what I had condemned him for not doing: I had to have integrity. I had to treat him the way I'd want to be treated.

I'd often heard that we are mirrors for each other. I now understand what that means. Sitting in the balcony of that drama now, I can clearly see that my ex-client and his buddy were merely mirroring my own hypocrisy. In living color, they dramatically demonstrated what it looks and feels like when someone says one thing and does something else.

They cast a spotlight on my own duplicity. They taught me that I can't publicly teach principles that claim that Life is always fair, God is never far, death is not The End and absolutely *nothing* is unforgivable, unless I live those principles. They taught me that I must respond to others' errors or misbehavior the same way that I would want someone to respond to mine: with unconditional forgiveness. They taught me to act as if Life is Round: Sow what I want to reap. Period.

I was the first person I forgave. It was my behavior that attracted these two souls into my experience. This was obviously the way they did business. I had to accept responsibility for attracting them into my business. My outcome was not their fault, so I sent them Light, Love and Forgiveness, and considered myself blessed, even though our encounter had created such financial turmoil that I was three months behind on my rent.

I was disturbed that nothing in my spirit compelled me to start packing. I didn't understand that; it was so out of character for me. I meditated, listening for direction. The message was always the same: Be still.

That didn't make sense. Time was running out. I needed to go before I was asked to leave. I waited for a different answer. None came.

My friend Vici, a Seattle-based minister, sent a collection of gospel songs to help me through that strange period. Among them was a favorite whose lyrics echoed my spirit's message: "When you've done all that you can, just stand."

I surrendered, released any claim to my apartment and my possessions and affirmed that the situation would be resolved perfectly. Every time those two businessmen crossed my mind, I stopped, forgave them and resumed packing, despite my inner resistance.

The day before the movers were scheduled, I called my landlady to advise her of my status.

"Give it another 30 days," she told me. "You never know what will happen in 30 days."

My knees literally buckled. I could hardly believe what this angel was saying. She and I had never met! She lived in another city; everything had always been handled by a realtor.

I began to understand why I had not felt compelled to pack. I began to believe that I was going to witness a miracle.

Nearly 30 days later, however, nothing had happened. Although my spirit had previously resisted and my body had not allotted enough time to get it all done, I quickly began to pack. Obviously, the perfect resolution to this situaion was for me to move on. I embraced that.

Suddenly, out of nowhere, a sizable project materialized. Unfortunately, time had run out. Then, just as suddenly, the day before my scheduled move, Vici called to check on me. She had been monitoring my situation closely and was glad to hear that I would soon be starting a big project with a reliable client.

She had offered several times to lend me the money I needed, but since I had nothing but empty promises of income, I had refused.

"Are you ready to accept the money now?" she asked. The next day, I received her check for almost $9,000.

It was my miracle, my blessing, and a beautiful ending to a wonderful lesson in forgiveness, trust and surrender.

I've learned during 20 years of carefully observing my own dramas and those of others that we respond to unpleasant situations in one of two ways: with fear or with faith. Those who believe that God is a man who resides in a far away place and periodically kills people to solve problems typically respond to challenges with fear and anger. They worry a lot. They believe that tragic things happen *to* them. It's difficult to surrender to God's way when we want things to turn out our way.

Those who see God as an ever-present, eternally loving and unconditionally forgiving spirit are more likely to respond to unpleasant situations with faith. They believe that everything happens for a reason—and a good one, at that. Situations—even tragic ones—are divinely ordered, and happen *for* them, not *to* them. No matter what things look like on the surface, each challenge presents an opportunity to trust God to resolve everything in the most perfect way and at the most perfect time, in the best interest of all parties.

I had made a powerful demonstration of faith, and I felt that I had cleared a major roadblock—but was it a fluke? I really wanted to strengthen my spiritual muscles.

Have you ever tried to acquire a new skill or learn a new sport? As you know, it's a process: We start as unconscious incompetents; we don't know what we don't know. We progress to conscious incompetence, when we discover what we don't know. From there, we graduate to conscious competence. We now know the steps or the rules, and by consciously applying them, we can use the skill or play the sport. Finally, we achieve the level of unconscious competence, and we can perform the task effortlessly, without even thinking about it.

My concern with much of the Law of Attraction material is that we're expected to achieve the level of unconscious competence without fully understanding or experiencing the full learning process.

Unless you're exceptionally gifted, there's only one way to reach the level of unconscious competence: practice, practice, practice. And there's only one way to consistently sow what we want to reap so that we can effortlessly attract what we desire: practice, practice, practice.

I think my soul was determined to master this ability, so it eventually attracted not just two, but a small army of souls to teach me. Many were highly skilled in the art of solving problems in ways that they would not want theirs to be solved. They were perfect!

Just like a good book that draws you into its plot, the characters were introduced onto my stage gradually, until my lovely cast was littered with a duplicitous actor here, a petty actor there, a vindictive one in the corner, an egomaniacal one, a couple of liars and a few garden variety snakes. *Talk about high drama!*

Some of them infuriated me so much that I instinctively fought back. How quickly I had forgotten that sowing retaliation reaps retaliation. Luckily, it was a brief memory lapse. I quickly focused on my script and for support, I called my Divine Director onto the stage.

The directions I received were powerful and profound: "Be still. When all is said and done, you will not be held accountable for the way others treated you."

Why didn't I think of that? I initially considered walking off the stage and out of their line of fire. But my Director said that staying in their crosshairs offered me the greatest opportunity to practice being Christlike, to act as if Life is round. That made sense. Virtuosos practice their crafts daily, devoting many hours to each session. I decided that I would, too. I wanted to be that good.

Months passed. The shady, mean-spirited actors kept plotting, and I kept practicing.

I wanted to be forgiven, so I forgave. I wanted to be blessed, so I blessed. I wanted to be consciously aware of the God presence in me, so I envisioned them full of the Light and Love of God, even though they probably could not see it in themselves. I wanted this behavior to become second nature, and I was grateful to them for giving me that opportunity.

In a "judge not, lest ye be judged" and "condemn not, lest ye be condemned" world, our responses matter; our responses attract: You kick me. I retaliate. Even if you limp away and never bother me again, I can count on one thing: At some point, I'm going to make a mistake and others are going to retaliate against me. Then they're going to attract someone who'll retaliate when they make mistakes. And on and on, in a vicious Self-to-Self circle.

It's one of the Law of Attraction secrets that no one wants to talk about. Like all laws, this law works the same way for 100% of the people, 100% of the time. We can test it by retaliating, or we can test it by forgiving.

I could see what chaos and pain I had attracted through my old habits. If I hoped to attract something different, I had to respond differently. If I hoped to reap a scrumptious harvest, I was going to have to weed my garden. I committed myself to doing that.

It didn't happen quickly, but I was in it to win it. Then, in the most perfect way and at the most perfect time, the curtain finally came crashing down on this drama—my signal that I had successfully gotten the insights that I'd come for, and I was free to leave the theater.

I bolted out of the door before anyone could scream, "encore!" What a glorious day! I felt as if I had successfully defended my doctoral thesis.

I had learned a rich, rewarding lesson. Better than that, I had mastered the art of stepping back and allowing others to learn theirs.

It helps to act with intention. We also must pay attention to what we're doing—and be aware of what we're attracting. For example:

- If you punish others when you decide that they have offended you, are you attracting *compassion* or *punishment* when you offend others?

- If you refuse to forgive someone, are you attracting *forgiveness* or *condemnation* when you make mistakes?

- If you treat others as if they are unlovable, are you attracting *loving* or *unloving* behavior into your experience?

- If you think that God favors you over others, are you attracting *discriminatory* or *equal* treatment?

- If you treat others unjustly, are you attracting those who will treat you *fairly* or *unfairly?*

It's no secret: Before we can consciously attract what we desire, we must understand how we unconsciously attract what we deserve. This is ancient wisdom, found in the book of the prolific Gentile physician, Luke:

"Judge not, and you will not be judged; condemn not, and you will not be condemned; forgive, and you will be forgiven." In other words, Life is round; you reap what you sow.

In many cases, the behavioral weeds we've unconsciously nurtured most of our lives are taking control of our garden, preventing our desired harvests from fully germinating. We've been growing those weeds for eons. How long will it take us to root them out?

We need to talk about that, because we're approaching the foot of the Unseen Bridge.

"Our task is to prepare
a vessel to be filled,
not to fill an imagined vessel
with what we dream
it has been prepared for."

Guy Finley
www.guyfinley.com

Secret #4

Either the Law Controls Your Outcomes—Or You Do

Many believe that our actions and desires can change who we are and what we attract into our lives. In reality, it's who we are that changes our actions, desires and what we attract into our life experiences.

Because most of us believe that we are mere mortals whose lives begin and end in a body, we tend to limit our desires to physical stuff, the slowly moving molecules that constitute creature comforts and other physical beings. It's as if we haven't noticed that nothing in the physical world lasts forever. Everything on Earth ages, deteriorates and dies—bodies as well as buildings. My goodness, birth is a terminal condition!

There is no eternal potential here, yet we focus all our energy on transitory physical manifestations and try to solve all our problems with physically limiting solutions.

The belief that the Law of Attraction was placed at our disposal to draw desired people and things into our lives and improve our physical conditions is just as curious a phenomenon. The Law's power and purpose are so much greater than that. Engaging it in such a limited way is like flying a jet to the local mall.

We have forgotten what the Law is and what it does, so we continue commanding it to produce everything from the mundane to the miraculous. We think we consciously attract things to us by visualizing every detail of our desired manifestations, claiming they are ours, and squealing with delight as we pretend that we've already achieved our goals by their deadlines.

It's a dramatic mental workout that nets inconsistent results. More often than not, our circumstances don't change, our cash doesn't begin to flow positively, our ideal mates don't materialize, and our health conditions don't improve upon our command.

At the risk of sounding cynical: If it's a law, shouldn't the opposite be true? If a thousand of us hold bricks in our hands directly over our feet, what will happen to all of us if we let go? I rest my case.

Ask any aeronautical engineer how much effort is required to defy the law of gravity. It's not simple to defy the Law of Attraction, either, and yet that's what many of us are trying to do. Either we've misunderstood this law or we've overestimated our power over laws.

The Law of Attraction is a simple reciprocal law: Whatever you do comes back to you. The Law responds unfailingly in the most perfect way (not necessarily the way we want), at the most perfect time (not always when we want), serving up what we have dished out and restoring our behaviors to their proper balance. If we are generous, we attract generosity. If we are unkind, we attract unkindness.

The Law delivers equity, as expressed in "an eye for an eye," "forgive us our trespasses *as* we forgive others," (or as *A Course in Miracles'* phrased it: "You accept God's forgiveness by extending it to others.")

The Law of Attraction is a simple and orderly spiritual law that cannot be manipulated. It is not going to weed through all of our behaviors and toss us only the stuff we desire. It also is not going to create chaos in the Universe by allowing us to trot our new wish lists to the front of the long line of old behaviors that have patiently waited weeks, months, years or even centuries to return to us at the most perfect time.

Just because we didn't know that we had been unconsciously stuffing the Law's jaws with desirable and undesirable behaviors doesn't mean that all of them haven't been digested and will not be regurgitated.

We seem to think that "what goes around comes around" applies to other people, not to us. That's the only explanation for treating others in ways that we would not want to be treated. If we remember that we are always creating our future experiences and that payback is always on the horizon, we would interact differently. But alas, we forget.

We could legitimately argue that these memory lapses really aren't our fault. After all, we learned many of our bad behaviors as children: We learned to "get even," show others who's boss. It was on the playground that we learned to be judgmental, condescending, unforgiving, cruel, punitive and combative, too. Our behaviors weren't simply reinforced; in many cases, they were rewarded when we scored what we thought were victories over others. *Wow, did that feel good!*

That was then. Now we have to consider the number of times since childhood that we've sown behaviors that we never wanted or intended to reap. Count back even farther if we are more than finite physical bodies!

What if our eternal souls have been making similar mistakes for eons? Those of you who've read *EARTH Is the MOTHER of All Drama Queens,* in which I sleuthed some of my own spiritual history, know how these behaviors can return to haunt us, even though our brains are not consciously aware of where our souls have been and what they've done.

The question is: What now? Is it our irreversible fate to reap every errant thought, belief and behavior we've ever sown?

No, it's not. And with all due respect to those who believe that God sadistically demands barbaric live sacrifices as a condition of forgiveness or as a consequence of human error, I ask you to consider the possibility that God is too big, too wonderful and too loving to commit homicide, genocide—or filicide.

These are considered evil crimes when perpetrated by humans. Why would we accept anyone's claims that God's conduct is so diabolical? It's not only illogical, it has proved harmful to the human spirit.

Our conflicting thoughts have caused us to pour new wine into old skins. It's a common error predating the Common Era.

Remember what happened when followers of a radical Jew embraced their teacher's empowering message that God is an unconditionally loving, forgiving, healing, nonjudgmental and omnipresent Spirit that is a Light within us? Instead of replacing their long-held belief that God is a dictatorial, threatening, punitive, murderous and judgmental male supreme being who lives as many light years away as Mount Olympus, they poured Jesus' vision of God directly on top of their religion's vision of God. As a result, they planted and watered a seed that produced a double-minded harvest. They gave us a God that:

※ Is invisible spirit—but has gender, body parts and the character flaws of the most reprehensible human beings;

※ Is sometimes unconditionally forgiving, sometimes vindictive and heals humans when He's not mortally wounding them in acts of inhumane retribution;

※ Is present everywhere—but lives "up there," so humans must do extraordinary things to be near Him, including believing unwaveringly that His behavior is patterned after that of mythical pagan gods;

❃ Created us, loves us unconditionally and, like the prodigal son's father, wants a relationship with us—but will allow only his favorites to return Home;

❃ Is unerring, but regretted creating humans, so destroyed them all because they were sinful by nature—then He created more humans who were, of course, sinful by nature; and

❃ Loves us and grants us free will to do anything we want, but will mercilessly torture us if we don't do precisely what He wants.

It's safe to say that if someone publicizes that he has murdered hundreds of thousands of people in fits of wrath and he commands others to solve problems that way, we generally don't want to share zip codes with him, let alone cultivate close relationships. We simply don't feel safe around anyone whose behavior swings from one extreme to another.

But, for whatever reason, we have made an exception in this case—perhaps because we believe that God will brutalize us, too, if we don't do as we're told or believe as we're told.

We've even adopted some of these inconsistent behaviors and mixed messages in our daily interactions. I recently heard an angry but reverent young man reacting to a perceived insult: "I'm not going to be vengeful," he insisted. "I'm going to ram those words down their throats with all the Christian love and charity that I can muster."

On another occasion, I overheard a man remarking to his friends, "I consider myself to be very religious; but if someone messes with my family, I don't care what God or anybody else says, I'm gonna kill 'em!"

Most of us say we believe that what goes around comes around, yet we don't connect the dots between ramming someone's words down his throat and subsequently attracting someone into our lives who will ram words down ours. We don't connect reacting violently with attracting violent reactions.

That's probably why our hearts get all aflutter when someone tells us that we can have whatever we want simply by holding positive thoughts and making demands on the Universe.

The burning question is: Can we make a discernible difference in our own lives? And if the Law of Attraction returns ALL of our actions to us, are we forever slaves of the

Ghost of Mistakes Past? It depends upon—you guessed it—what you believe and how you act. If you believe in a controlling, vindictive God, you probably shouldn't have any real expectation that you can effect any changes in your life, relationships or circumstances. Your beliefs simply will not allow it.

After all, your God is controlling, dictatorial and forceful. He makes demands, threatens and punishes harshly. As a consequence, fear has a controlling influence on your thoughts and behaviors. Creating positive change in your life would be a great challenge.

Force and control are the polar opposites of love and freedom. Those who mimick the behaviors of a forceful God tend to be manipulative. They don't empower others; in fact, they feel threatened by empowered people, so they rule and manage others through fear, intimidation and condescension. They judge, belittle and punish. They hurt.

As mental processes expert Dr. David R. Hawkins outlined in his profound book *Power vs. Force,* it's easy to distinguish forceful people from their powerful counterparts. Powerful people are utterly fearless. They aren't threatened by anything or anyone, and they don't have the desire or need to control others. Powerful people can give love unconditionally, and they easily support others' empowerment and freedom of choice.

If we truly believe that God is forceful, controlling and punitive, no amount of positive thinking, creative visualizations or emotional projection can counteract our underlying feelings of victimization, powerlessness and fear. How can we be in control if we believe that we are being controlled?

Fearful people attract fearful people. The results can be catastrophic. Fear drives the behaviors of those who are controlled as much as it drives those who control them. The controlled are more likely to consider themselves victims, they cower with heads bowed and eyes cast downward. They are unable to see the Big Picture. They think they are small and are more likely to do small things. They ask for little and manifest less.

By contrast, those who are in touch with their eternal nature tend to see farther, think bigger and act stronger. They view situations within broader contexts, they create in more enlightened and evolved ways. They don't limit their desires to small things such as physical manifestations. Why would they, when they can see so much more?

When we are in touch with the reality of our eternity, it's easier to see that every experience we have has a purpose. Instead of focusing on attracting physical objects, we can ask for spiritual insights, answers and guidance so we can fulfill that purpose and grow through the lessons each experience provides us. The irony is that the residue of this higher-level thinking typically manifests into physical riches—not just money, but peace of mind, inner joy, creature comforts and loving relationships.

It calls to mind a story about a legendary rabbi who not only believed that the eternal Spirit of God was within him, he believed that this Spirit was who he really was: He was one with It because It is All There Is. He believed that we, too, are one with It because It is All There Is. Whatever we do to the least of our brothers, he said, we also do to him, because there is only One Presence in the Universe.

Jesus's profound wisdom and empowering messages attracted many followers. Twelve men were said to have been particularly dedicated to him, and accompanied him throughout his travels.

One day the group reportedly encountered a beggar by the roadside. After learning that the man had been visually impaired at birth, the disciples were curious. Based on the teachings of their religion, it appeared that the beggar's condition was punishment for sin. Was it his parents' sin, they asked their rabbi, or his own?

Since there is no evidence that sins can be committed in the womb, the only way a newborn could have been punished for his sin was if he had committed it in a different body at a different time. This meant that these men believed in an eternal spirit that transited from one physical body into another.

Jesus's response urged his followers to think bigger, beyond physical appearances and far beyond their belief in divine retribution (an oxymoron, if ever there was):

"Neither he nor his parents sinned," he said. "It is so that the works of God might be made visible through him." (John 9:3)

Notice that he didn't say, "Come on, you know Life is unfair. Why would you ask me something like that?" He said that the man's condition served a higher purpose.

If we dared to think bigger and dig deeper, we'd see that our own adversities have also served a higher purpose. What lessons would we have missed without those adverse experiences, if Life had not grabbed our attention or made us cry out for God's help? What great insights could we have gained if we had not judged or been distracted by the situation?

One person's curse is another person's blessing. It's a matter of perspective.

Reflecting on the lesson that the disciples learned, think of the opportunities that one person's impairment provides for others. How would we learn compassion, generosity, supportiveness or patience if there was no one who needed it, no one who inspired it? If we don't label a situation as "good luck" or a "bad break," we might be able to see it for what it is: an opportunity to grow, give, receive or learn. It's our choice.

What if God was powerful enough to have granted us the freedom to do whatever we chose? Imagine that before we ran outside out to play on planet Earth, we were given a few simple suggestions, since the all-knowing and eternally loving God wanted to spare us any unpleasant consequences arising from the reciprocal spiritual Law of Attraction.

They weren't complicated suggestions, and there were only a handful. Like bread crumbs to help us find our way home, reminders of these tips were scattered about in various places. It would be impossible for anyone to miss them. And if we heeded these simple suggestions, we would be able to powerfully leverage the Law of Attraction in pleasant ways.

Perhaps you recall encountering these tips somewhere along your path:

Leveraging the Law

- Do unto others as you would have them do unto you;

- Love yourself, your neighbors and your enemies;

- Judge nothing, condemn no one; and

- Forgive seventy times seven.

When you are consciously aware that whatever you do will be done to you, you tend to make different choices. You don't hurt others, you don't steal, you don't lie, you don't hate, disrespect, cheat, control or threaten. You honor your vows. You don't treat others in ways that you would not want to be treated.

We have forgotten these simple suggestions. We slipped into these confining costumes called human bodies, got so caught up in all the physical life drama that we forgot about reality. We thought that the Earth stage was real life. We thought that we could do hurtful things and win life's wars, simply because we won some battles.

If we didn't judge situations and people as "good" or "bad," we would be able to clearly see the Divine Energy—and Divine Value—in everything and everyone. We would instinctively uplift, not condescend to others. We would be more honest—especially with ourselves.

What if we were more forgiving and less vengeful? What if we didn't relish others' failures or shortfalls? What if we saw ourselves and others as less mortal and more divine? What if we could cross the Unseen Bridge and consistently create our desired outcomes?

As with any bridge, there are weight restrictions on this one. You're going to have to get rid of some of the baggage that is bulging with misperceptions of who you are and what God is. These beliefs are reflected in the way you treat others, and in other behaviors that attract physical, emotional and financial discomfort into your life.

How do you do that? Try the "F" word: Yep, forgive. Forgiveness transforms everything. It makes every relationship and every soul new. Forgiveness lightens your load; it gives you a fresh start. It frees you from the back-breaking chains of resentment and anger.

Where do you start? Well, everything starts with Self; forgiveness is no exception.

Don't try to remember every mistake you've made; that would be impossible. Plus, you certainly don't want to spend days or years dwelling on negative stuff. Simply forgive yourself for everything you've ever done in your entire existence that might have attracted unpleasant circumstances.

Opportunities abound to use the "F" word with reckless abandon. You might even want to make a game of it. That's what I did.

When I decided to seriously practice forgiveness, a host of karma-creating creatures magically appeared to support me, like my client who signed that one-year contract that he couldn't honor.

"F" him! Yep, I forgave him. Ditto for his buddy who also didn't honor his word. "F" both of them in super-sized helpings with unlimited refills. *Ooh! That was so satisfying!*

Even now, whenever they cross my mind, I bless them. I've done it so much that I notice that I say it with loving sincerity, even sympathy. I actually feel sorry for them because I understand the reciprocal Law of Attraction. I have forgiven them completely, so that I will never again attract souls like them or the hurtful circumstances they bring.

Forgiving everyone, including yourself, for random acts of unkindness is not for punks.

That's why I decided to make it a game.

Our minds can create anything, so in the blink of an eye, I created the world's largest coliseum—state-of-the-art, of course. The concession stands sold delicious food at reasonable prices. It had plush seats, cup holders cradling beautiful crystal champagne glasses, and under each chair was a mysterious looking sheet of shiny metal.

Satisfied that I had created a first class venue, I closed my eyes and called forth participants in every encounter in my eternal life that still held some residual anger, guilt, judgment, condemnation or resentment because I had never said or thought the "F" word. Instantly, the stadium was filled with the actors who were pivotal to each of those scenes. The place was packed!

In fact, there were so many folks clustered in the parking lot that I had to build an adjacent stadium! Who knew I had created so many hurt-filled relationships over my eternal lifetime?

The air was buzzing with anticipation—curiosity mostly, but I could sense a bit of hostility, too. Some folks obviously had hoped never to see me again. Others were embarrassed and ashamed to look at me.

I smiled, took a deep breath, and lowered the gigantic four-sided screens that hung over each stadium. As the lights dimmed and music slowly faded in, I explained that we were about to witness the most amazing reality show ever. A hush went over the crowd.

Moments later, in the severely edited version of my eternal life, many in the audience saw themselves on-screen, co-starring in scenes that had no entertainment value; however they were extremely valuable to all of us.

What we witnessed on the big screen was "whatever you do comes back to you," in living color. We saw the same souls playing different roles during different time periods, and they were repeating similar interactions until those situations were healed. We saw evidence that every thought, every action, and every word leave dark impressions on our eternal souls and impact our future experiences and relationship dynamics.

It was spellbinding, eye-opening stuff. We were mesmerized. Watching the scenes, it was so clear why Jesus had said of his torturers, "Forgive them, Father, for they know not what they do." Jesus knew what they were doing to themselves by brutalizing him. He fully understood the reciprocal spiritual Law of Attraction. He probably felt sorry for them.

Stunned silence greeted the movie's end. Not one soul moved.

Perfect! I didn't want them to. (That's the great thing about directing your own mental movie.) I asked my guests to lift the glasses in their cup holders. Instantly, they were filled with pink champagne.

I lifted my glass, bowed humbly to each section of the stadium, and did what I should have done ages ago: I said the "F" word.

I forgave them and I forgave myself for anything I might have done to hurt anyone in any way. I followed with the "L" word, telling them that I loved each of them the way Jesus taught us to love, the way God loves all prodigal children: unconditionally.

In an instant, our hurtful encounters were healed. We saluted each other and sipped the delicious bubbly.

Oops! I had forgotten something. "Please pick up the iridescent sheet that is under your seat and hold it high," I instructed them.

I didn't even know what was going to happen, frankly. So we were all surprised when the forgiveness that I had gently cast their way reflected off of those panels right back at me.

Oh. My. God! The powerful energy of forgiveness bounced off every panel, multiplied and intensified.

There was joy in the house—and ecstasy in our hearts! We watched the spirit of forgiveness transform the darkness of anger and resentment that had been our burden for a very long time. It became a massive ball of pure light, rose out of the stadium, then disappeared into absolute nothingness.

The cheers were deafening. We were free, thank God Almighty! We were finally released from our self-imposed prisons.

When I awoke from my dream, I could still feel the overwhelming joy, the chills from that experience. I had witnessed a miracle.

I could physically feel that I had removed roadblocks from my life path that had hampered my progress, created unhappy relationships, and had attracted people who treated me in ways that they would not want to be treated. Something had changed. I certainly had changed.

Now, when I find myself in a jam, the first thing I do is "F" it! In fact, I make a grand production of it. I write the most powerful, life-altering script. It has only one scene and one line that I deliver most dramatically: "I forgive..."

What about you? Look in the mirror, make eye contact and say out loud, "I forgive myself for everything I've ever done in my entire existence that has caused others pain and, consequently, has caused me pain. I forgive myself for not remembering that with every thought, every belief and every act, I am triggering the Law of Attraction."

Say it and mean it. If emotions rise, let them. Spend some time in that forgiving space until your Light is no longer hiding under a bushel.

Forgive yourself for every time that you've judged, condemned or been spiteful to someone. Forgive yourself for all the occasions that you "got even"—or wanted to. Forgive yourself for all those times that you were uncharitable or unkind. Forgive yourself for each instance that you were not authentic or honorable, and every time throughout all time that you lied, cheated and took something that didn't belong to you. Replace the darkness of those errant thoughts and actions with Light. Just "F" it!

Release yourself from the consequences of angry outbursts, exerting force, gossiping and mentally or physically battering someone. Forgive yourself for believing the unbelievable, things that created distance between you and your Divine Self, things that generated fear and created more drama in your life.

Forgive every negative thought you've ever had. Just "F" it.

Forgive yourself for treating others in ways that you would not want to be treated—and for attracting people into your life who treated you in ways that they would not want to be treated. And please don't forget to forgive yourself for all the times that you refused to forgive others or made them wait or suffer until you decided that you wanted to forgive them. Forgive yourself for believing that this act of smallness made you bigger.

Forgive yourself until you actually feel forgiven. Don't simply believe it, know that you are forgiven. Know that God loves you and forgives you unconditionally, no matter what you've said or done—or what you have believed that God has done.

Let yourself off the hook. You have been conditioned to believe in things and act in ways that did not serve your Highest Good. Surely, if you had known better, you would have done better. God knows that.

Once you've forgiven yourself, forgive everyone throughout your eternal life who has ever treated you unkindly. Forgive them. Forgive them and forgive them again. If they had known better, they would have done better, too.

Forgiving someone doesn't mean that you have to embrace that person or ever spend any time with him or her again. Forgiveness is an act of release. Do you really want to weigh yourself down by holding onto people who hurt others? Do you want to carry them in your mind by harboring resentment? Do you want to hurt yourself by wishing ill upon them or gloating because they got their "comeuppance?"

Let them go. You're only creating the opportunity for resentment to come your way through the reciprocal Law of Attraction. Being mad at them doesn't hurt them, it hurts you. Let it go. Clean out the clutter, all the errant behaviors that have blocked the speedy delivery of your deepest desires. Move on, as if the drama never happened. In reality, it didn't.

Forgiveness will enable you to step onto the Unseen Bridge, and it will guide you, unencumbered, safely across. Once on the other side, you will be keenly aware of how the Law of Attraction works, and you will consciously plant seeds that heal yourself and others. You will be in control of what you attract into your life, in a much more powerful way than others have described.

Controlling your outcomes has often been mistaken for the curious practice of "claiming" things. How many times has someone told me, "Just claim it, girl!"

To me, it's like the tail wagging the dog. Everything I want is not intended for me or in my best interest. My life purpose is not the same as someone else's, neither are the lessons I came here to learn, so our earthly experiences, relationships and possessions will naturally be different.

If you are compelled to claim something, how about claiming that your will is in alignment with the will of your Divine Self? Claim that you will discover what your purpose and your lessons are. Claim that you will step back and let the inner Light of God lead you.

When you do that, and you encounter those who have forgotten who they are and how they should treat others, you will understand why they have appeared. They came because your soul called them. They came so that they could fulfill your soul's desire to make forgiveness a new habit, a knee-jerk reaction, an instinct.

Typically, when we learn new concepts, particularly spiritual ones, we grasp them intellectually, but that's as far as it goes. Your soul wants the lessons to move from your head to your heart, so you will notice that some situations—generally painful ones—keep repeating until you respond differently, until you apply the lessons in a practical way, until you remember that God is within you and until you consistently allow your God Self to lead your actions and interactions.

Sometimes situations masquerade as adversity. They are not. They are not setbacks or punishments. They came to grow you up. They are practice exercises—and practice makes perfect, Loved One.

You *want* to practice remembering. You want to practice forgiveness. You want to become proficient at experiencing situations without judging them or feeling victimized or paralyzed by them.

You want to learn the lessons those situations were created to teach you. You want your blessing. You want to reach the stage of unconscious competence so that you can activate the Law of Attraction in a positive way. You want to control what comes back to you so that there will be no unpleasant surprises.

That way, when folks bearing pain show up, you won't be angry or afraid, you'll simply be curious. You'll instinctively ask the all-knowing part of yourself: "What is this beautiful soul here to teach me? How is this soul going to help me to grow?" Don't resent them, be grateful that they came.

The only way you will learn to instinctively forgive is to take advantage of every opportunity to choose forgiveness. Do not concern yourself with whether others will get what they deserve. You are not the boss of their karma. The Law of Attraction knows its job, and it doesn't need your help.

When all is said and done, you will not be held accountable for the way others treated you, so when you're angry, when you're afraid, when you're frustrated, when you pray, when you want to scream, try this: Ask for the situation to be resolved for the Highest Good of all concerned. Then let it go. Trust God's integrity and you won't have to rely on anyone else's.

Remember, what goes around does come around. Every eternal soul has its inescapable circle of attraction. Do you want to focus your attention on someone else's circle, or would your time be better spent monitoring yours?

Speaking of circles, I have another little game to suggest: There will be times when you'll be so irritated that you'll feel the urge to thrust a finger at someone. Whatever finger you choose, use it instead to draw a circle in the air. That circle will help to remind you that Life is round and that you can control what circles back to you on the spiritual wings of the Law of Attraction.

Teach this little game to your children, grandchildren and students so that they can learn very early how to control what returns to them through the Law of Attraction. You can change their worlds, you can heal their souls. You have the power to stop the darkness before it overwhelms them.

We teach what we are learning and, believe me, we are all lifelong students. We must maintain loving vigilance over our thoughts, beliefs and actions to ensure that we have fully recovered from our old addictions, the old habits of responding negatively to situations and treating others the way that we've been told that God treats us.

With practice, you will be ready to take action when someone whispers an ancient secret in your ear. You will be ready to practice at the level of unconscious competence.

Until you understand who you are, what you believe and how your beliefs impact your behavior, you run the risk of pouring new wine into old skins when you experiment with Law of Attraction techniques.

Focus first on creating inner peace, then seek a path of eternal Truth. Choose whichever path you like: Prayer, meditation, church, synagogue, mosque, books, seminars, retreats, audios, creative visualizations and a variety of other spiritual tactics will support you in remembering who you are and how to create more powerfully. Journaling, art, music, even silence can inspire your creativity.

Instead of visualizing every detail of a physical object that you desire, try seeing the Light of God that is within you. What does it look like? Is it a small spark? Does it pulsate or vibrate?

Ask it to grow. See if it will fill every cell in your entire body and erase every dark crevice. What does that feel like?

Can you imagine that this Light is who you really are? Can you create through its power and wisdom and not from your physical brain?

Remember that there is no spot where God is not. Do not judge your path, and forgive those who do. They will judge until they grow.

It calls to mind a mega-church minister who lost all but a few in his congregation when he had the revelation that God is good all the time—and all the time, God is good. When he told his flock that God would not cast someone into hell, thousands fled en masse to worship with a minister who would tell them otherwise, someone who would say that Satan has power and that God will brutally torture those who doesn't believe that.

These souls didn't understand the implications of their beliefs. They didn't even do the elementary-school math: If Satan has even the tiniest fraction of power, it means that God does not have it all. It means that they believe in a Some-Mighty, not Almighty God.

Do these well-meaning but fearful people really believe that God is not omnipotent? Probably not. Do they believe that God is a sadist? I doubt it, nevertheless they wanted to stay in their fearful comfort zone rather than venture into the Loving Light.

All is well. We are all seekers. Whatever we seek, we shall find. Seek Truth.

Your life and all of Life are open books. Dare to read them. Dare to understand who you really are and what God is. Dare to explore your beliefs. Everything you need to know is within you. Open a dialogue. It will lovingly tell you anything you need to know. Call upon it to help you discern ancient books. Flip through some pages of mythology, and don't be surprised if you hear yourself say, "I knew that! I just forgot."

Remember, you have only one life to live—and it is Eternal.

I love you as God loves you:
Unconditionally.
Pat

www.ingramcontent.com/pod-product-compliance
Ingram Content Group UK Ltd.
Pitfield, Milton Keynes, MK11 3LW, UK
UKHW041419180426
11947UKWH00007B/221